Going

by Frankie Hartley
illustrated by Natalia Vasquez

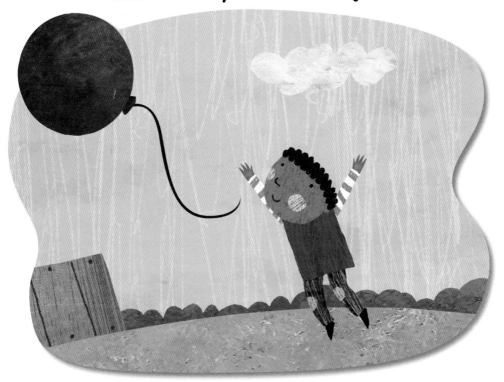

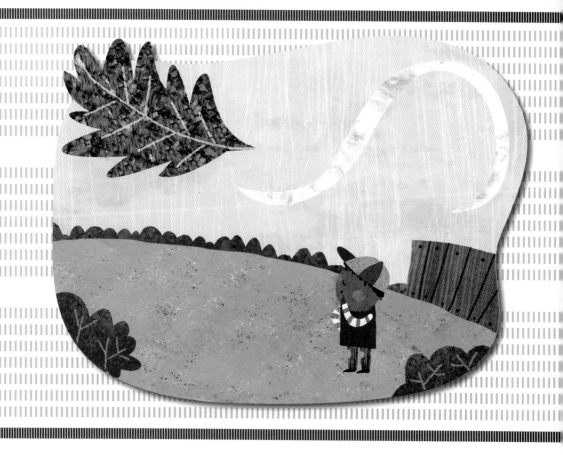

This leaf can go up.

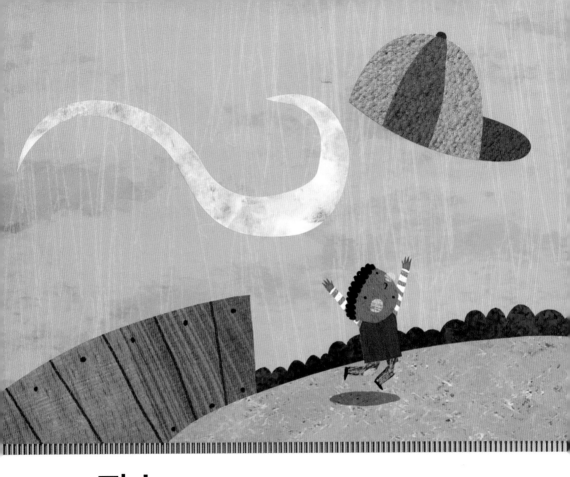

This cap can go up.

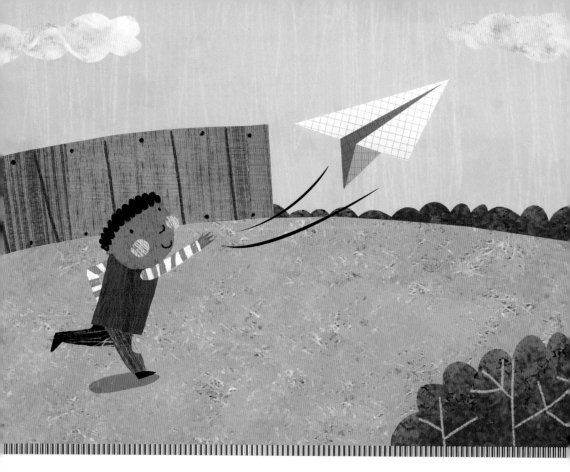

This plane can go up.

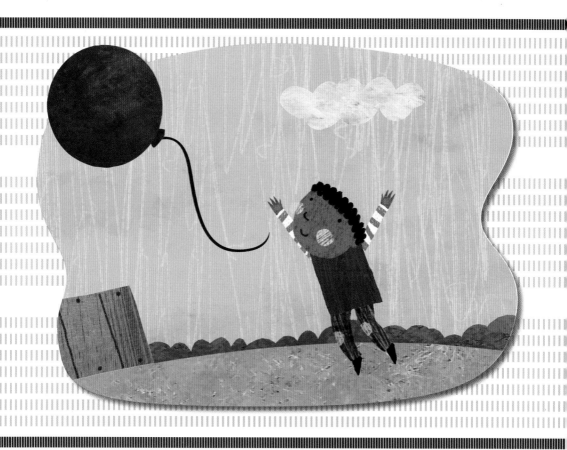

This balloon can go up.

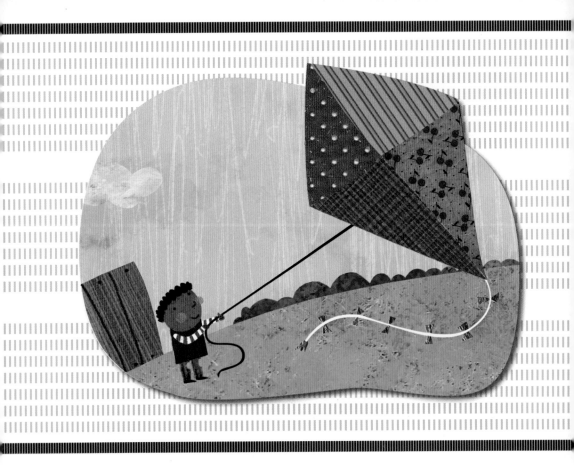

This kite can go up.

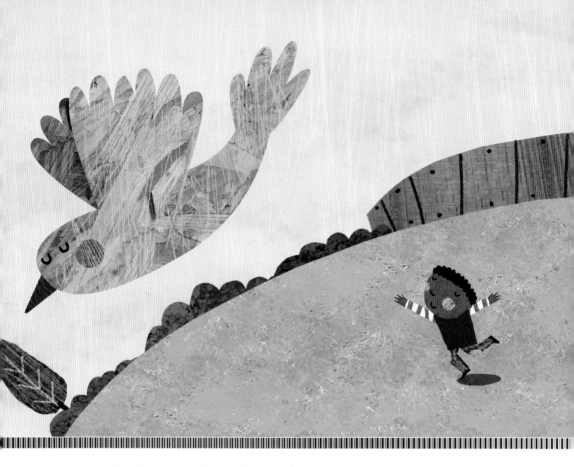

This bird can go up.

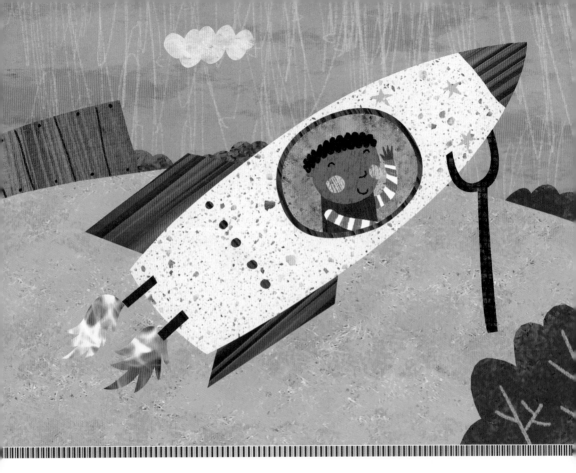

This rocket can go up.